ASSISI EMBROIDERY
Old Italian Cross-stitch Designs

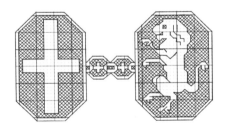

ASSISI EMBROIDERY
Old Italian Cross-stitch Designs

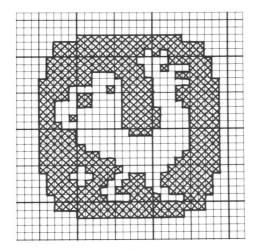

Eva Maria Leszner

B.T. Batsford Ltd, London

First published in Britain 1988 by B.T. Batsford Ltd
© Eva Maria Leszner 1988

ISBN 0 7134 5595 0

Typeset by Tek-Art Ltd, Kent and printed in Great Britain by
Anchor Brendon, Tiptree, Essex, for the publishers
B.T. Batsford Ltd 4 Fitzhardinge Street London W1H 0AH

Translation by Andrew Shackleton

CONTENTS

St Francis of Assisi preaches to the birds
– a fresco by Giotto in St Francis's Basilica in Assisi

INTRODUCTION

Assisi embroidery is a special form of cross-stitch work. It uses a method known as voiding, in which the background is embroidered instead of the design. The pattern which remains is then outlined in a darker colour in Holbein stitch to give it extra definition. The motifs which are used consist almost exclusively of symmetrically arranged animal pairs, mostly birds. The main motif and the cross-stitch background are surrounded with filigree scrollwork in Holbein stitch.

Both the designs and the techniques are based on an ancient Italian tradition stretching far back into the Middle Ages, which was revived in Assisi around the turn of this century.

2

ASSISI

Let us first consider the town itself. Assisi lies in the province of Umbria in central Italy. Umbria is one of the few Italian regions which is cut off from the sea; it forms an undulating basin interspersed with many hills, dips and winding valleys. The west of the region rises into the Apennine mountain range, where medieval towns nestle high up above the fertile valleys. The rich pasture land was famous in ancient times, since when the region has been commonly known as 'green Umbria'. The province still relies heavily on its agriculture, together with handicrafts and tourism.

The town of Assisi is world famous as the birthplace of San Francesco or St Francis of Assisi. As any guidebook will tell you, the town has 'scarcely had any history worth speaking of, either before or since'. The founder of the Franciscan Order was born in Assisi in 1182, and died here in 1226. The town is dominated by a mighty fortress, and clings to the slopes of Mount Subasio, from whose pinkish stone its Romanesque houses and churches are built. It is still surrounded by ancient ramparts, as at the time of St Francis.

The Franciscan Order expanded very fast, spreading well beyond the Alps. Even within Francis' lifetime there were more than 5,000 monks in the order, and by the time he was declared a saint in 1228, the town had become an important place of pilgrimage. About thirty years after the saint's death, two monastic churches were built in the Gothic style – one dedicated to St Francis and the other to St Clare, the founder of the Franciscan Order of Nuns. Assisi is a highly religious community, but has always remained small, and today has a population of about thirty thousand. Pilgrims have admittedly become fewer and fewer, but the number of tourists has increased correspondingly. And Assisi remains today as it has been for 800 years: the town of St Francis.

FRANCIS OF ASSISI

What were the teachings that made this man so famous? The son of a cloth merchant, he willingly devoted himself to a life of humility, obedience and above all poverty. In the times in which he lived, this was considered quite monstrous, even provocative, for the church of his time was anything but spiritual, and its kingdom was very much of this world. Bishops were also powerful local rulers, and lived in wealth and splendour off the fat of the land. And now here was someone who not only preached poverty, but practised it too.

Just as Christ gathered his disciples, so Francis gathered round him a group of like-minded souls to found the first of the orders of mendicant friars. These monks, St Francis foremost among them, were dressed literally in sackcloth and ashes – a brown cowl with just a cord for a belt. Their attitude to life was not one of penitence, but one of cheerfulness and joy in working to please God. They modelled their lives on the words of the Sermon on the Mount: '. . . they sow not, neither do they reap . . . yet your heavenly Father feedeth them'. St Francis is often represented in the company of animals, and many of the legends that have grown up around him are concerned with how he rescued animals in need. But the best-known of all is the story of how he preached to the birds. He apparently thought of himself as a brother to all God's creatures, not only to humans but to animals too; and when he met a whole flock of twittering birds, he is supposed to have preached to them. Just as in all legends, the birds understood what he was saying, and listened in silence and without fear; they did not fly away until he had finished preaching, whereupon they scattered in all directions. Francis preached the same ideas to them as he did to people – that they should praise God for the freedom and the life which he has given them.

TRADITIONAL EMBROIDERY

Although St Francis was the son of a rich cloth merchant, it would be presumptuous to imagine that this mendicant friar had anything to do with traditional Italian needlework! So it is best to make a clean break here before moving on to what is a completely separate chapter in Italian history.

White work flourished throughout Central and Northern Europe, especially in monastic communities, between the thirteenth and fifteenth centuries; but it was virtually unknown in Italy, and remains so to this day. In these sunnier climes, embroidery was done in bright, cheerful colours, even in the religious communities. Sacred embroidery was worked in split stitch, using coloured silk thread on a gold background. In the thirteenth and fourteenth centuries, a few monasteries developed a rather more modest style of embroidery, which in the sixteenth century flourished and spread into the secular community. The designs and motifs were voided on fine linen cloth, while the contours and the background were embroidered in coloured silk. First the outlines were drawn on the cloth, and then the contours of the designs were embroidered in simple running stitch or back stitch, using brown or black silk for religious embroidery. Then the whole of the background was filled in using red, green or yellow filling stitches. Normally long-armed cross stitch was used for this purpose, but there are traditional examples of backgrounds in openwork or chessboard filling stitch.

In secular embroidery, the motifs were based on the grotesques, satyrs, demons and ancient mythical beasts which had become popular during the Renaissance. In sacred embroidery, however, the motifs were more strongly influenced by traditional designs using bird or animal pairs

3

Two pieces of sixteenth century Italian silk embroidery on linen cloth, from the Museo-Nationale in Florence

surrounded by elaborate scrollwork. Such designs were already to be found on the stone reliefs and carved wooden choir stalls in Romanesque churches. They presumably came into Italian needlework via the silk trade. Silk manufacture had been introduced from Byzantium in the twelfth century; it first gained a foothold in Sicily, and from there spread to Florence, Lucca and Venice.

In the fifteenth century, Perugia, a town only 20 miles from Assisi, became a cotton manufacturing centre, producing white handkerchiefs, tablecloths and napkins woven with wide blue stripes. These stripes were again decorated with paired bird and animal motifs, voided in white against the blue background.

In the eighteenth and nineteenth centuries, all these weaving and embroidery techniques fell into oblivion, and the designs and motifs disappeared with them.

ASSISI EMBROIDERY

On 4 October 1902, St Francis's Day, St Anne's Convent in Assisi established the *Laboratorio Ricreativo Festivo Femminile San Francesco di Assisi* – a handicrafts workshop for poor girls in the town 'who wish to learn the art of embroidery'. The initiative for this came not from Assisi itself, but as part of a movement which had begun in 1870 in the town of Burano near Venice. The new state of Italy had been founded in 1861, and a group of noble ladies had 'for patriotic reasons' set themselves the task of rediscovering and reviving the traditional handicrafts. Their actions were also intended to help poor women to supplement the income of their families with paid work.

Political considerations may have been a primary motivating force: colonial wars were proving a burden on the country's economy, and taxes on flour were especially punitive to the poor; the progress of industrialization was considerably behind that of countries in Northern Europe, and the new monarchy was having to cope with much internal unrest.

But whatever the motives involved, the aim was to revive local traditions rather than to introduce new crafts from elsewhere. Assisi appears to have had no local secular traditions, so nothing could have been more natural in this religious-minded town than to rely on the legacy of their church past, combing the town's many monastic communities for traditional designs for the women to use in their work.

They took the traditional embroidery techniques and simplified them. Silk thread gave way to embroidery cotton; the outlines and contours were no longer drawn freely on to the cloth, but were counted out individually stitch by stitch; the background was embroidered in simple cross stitch; and the designs were if necessary simplified. These designs had been culled from sacred embroidery, and sometimes taken directly from the stone reliefs and and the wooden choirstalls in the churches. Particularly interesting was the way in which the complicated arabesque designs which surrounded the motifs were reduced to simple scrollwork patterns that could easily be counted stitch by stitch.

If you look at the designs, you will notice that bird motifs are by far the most common. Perhaps the women were thinking of St Francis himself when they included so many bird motifs in their collections. They made no changes at all in the colours they used. From the very beginning, they used

A door arch on the Basilica San Rufino in Assisi

5

the traditional red, blue, green or gold for the background, and black or brown for the outlines.

One further modification was needed: the traditional embroidery had been used purely for religious purposes, whereas what was now required was something that could be sold commercially. So instead of altar cloths and chasubles they made tablecloths and napkins. The women thus developed three basic design models that have since become just as characteristic of Assisi embroidery as the embroidery technique and the traditional motifs. The three basic models were medallion cloths (figs 84-90), cloths with decorated corners (figs 74-83) and cloths with scrollwork borders (figs 84-90). Each of them can be varied to include a vast range of different motifs, and the size can be modified to fit any size of cloth you may required.

The extraordinary success which Assisi embroidery has enjoyed can perhaps be attributed to the spirit of the age for which it was developed,

A gravestone from the Museo Communale in Pavia

6

or possibly to the marvellous organization which has gone into the sale of the finished goods, or to the large number of foreigners who have visited the town. All these factors have played their part. But the main reason for its success lies in the careful thought that has gone into the designs and in the outstanding workmanship that they reveal.

It is certainly true that the work of the training workshop at the convent soon developed into a flourishing home industry, which was to be found throughout the region. The designs quickly spread, not only to other Italian provinces, but to the whole of Europe and even overseas. Everywhere women began to embroider in the special style developed in Assisi, so that this newly resurrected Italian embroidery technique soon became known quite simply as Assisi embroidery. Up to the 1930s, all so-called 'genuine' articles – that is, those which had actually been embroidered in Assisi – were marked in the bottom right-hand corner with the cross of St Francis and the arms of the town of Assisi.

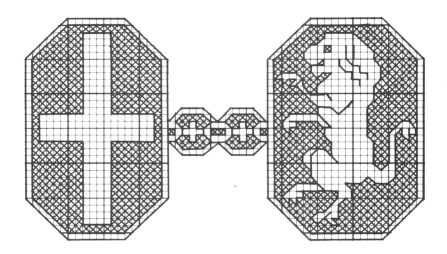

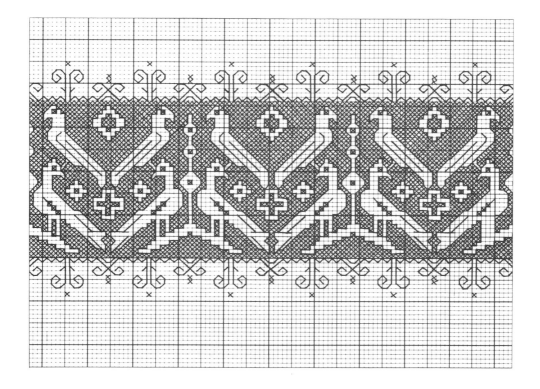

WORKING METHOD

Assisi embroidery is one of those satisfying techniques which require much less work than would appear to be the case. A wide decorative border in which the whole of the background is embroidered looks like a lot of work. But experience shows that it is not the large areas but the intricate little corners that take a long time to embroider. Fortunately there are not too many of these in Assisi embroidery.

THE BACKGROUND

Like other forms of cross-stitch work, Assisi embroidery can be worked on all types of evenweave fabrics – that is, materials which have the same number of warp and weft (vertical and horizontal) threads to the inch or centimetre. If the weave is irregular, then the cross stitches will not be square and the design will be distorted. The medieval embroidery was worked in minute stitches on very fine linen. Today, evenweave linen, hardanger, aida and even some furnishing fabrics can be used – the latter often have some synthetic content and, provided the weave is even, can be ideal for tablecloths, napkins and other regularly laundered items. With wall hangings or pictures, the overall effect is more important than fine detail, so the stitches can afford to be larger, and hopsack or hessian (burlap) may be suitable to work on.

EMBROIDERY THREADS

The traditional religious embroidery was worked using silk thread, but in Assisi embroidery cotton was used from the very beginning when the craft was revived. Stranded cotton (US: six-strand embroidery floss) is the most useful, since it can be divided into smaller threads as required. The thickness of thread you use will depend both on the fineness of the fabric and on how many threads each individual stitch is worked over. For example, on an evenweave linen that has 10 threads to 1 cm (25 threads to 1 in.), I might stitch over two threads of the weave at a time, using three strands for the cross-stitch and only two for the Holbein stitch. Wool thread can be used for embroidering on hessian (burlap) or other coarse cloths. For household items requiring frequent laundering, make sure the thread you use is colourfast.

NEEDLES AND FRAME

Like all cross-stitch work, Assisi embroidery should be worked using a blunt needle so as to avoid splitting the fibres of the background. A sharper needle may be easier to use, however, for sewing in the loose ends on the wrong side of the work.

Cross-stitch work is often done using a frame mounted on a table. Here the needle is held in the right hand above the fabric and passed to the left hand beneath. But I personally do cross stitch and Assisi embroidery with the fabric draped over my left hand, using my left index finger to guide the thread – I find I can work faster that way. I have seen professionals in Assisi do it both ways, some of them working with a frame and some without. It is best to try both methods, to see which suits you. If you embroider without a frame, you should touch the embroidery as little as possible, as it otherwise tends to lose its sheen and quickly becomes rather grubby.

EMBROIDERY TECHNIQUE

There are three elements to Assisi embroidery:
(*i*)   the outlines and detail of the designs;
(*ii*) the cross-stitch background;
(*iii*) the filigree scrollwork which forms the border decoration above and below the motifs, or on larger works connects the cross-stitch designs.
There are only two kinds of stitch used: Holbein stitch for the outlines and scrollwork, and cross stitch for the background.

In the sixteenth century, *Holbein stitch* was also very popular in Germany. It owes its rather nice name to the painter Hans Holbein the Younger, whose paintings show many clothes beautifully embroidered in this particular stitch. The technical terms for it is *double running stitch*. For this, first embroider along the outline in a row of simple running stitches of equal size; then return along the same line, filling in the spaces between the first row of stitches as in fig. 7, making sure that the thread passes through the same holes in the material as before. The Holbein stitches must be of the same size as the cross stitches of the background. Thus if each of the cross stitches is worked over two threads of the fabric, then each of the running stitches must be worked over two threads as well.

Cross stitch is worked in horizontal rows of diagonal stitches. As fig. 8 shows, you first embroider a full row of half crosses from left to right, then

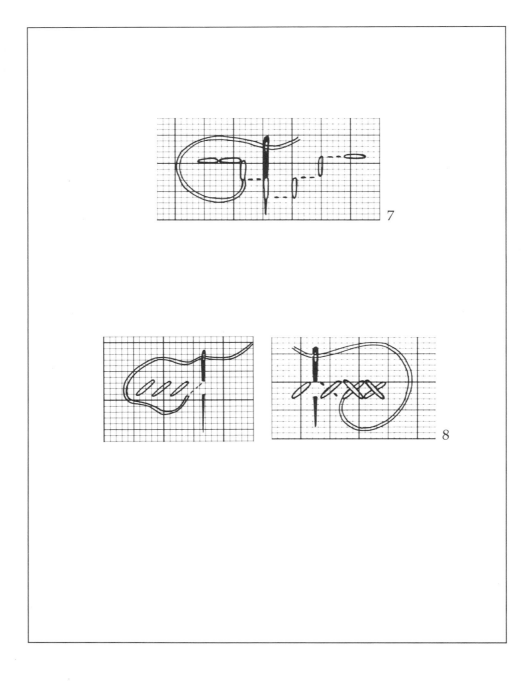

7

8

return from right to left, completing the crosses as you go. Repeat the process row by row, always making sure that the needle passes from the top to the bottom of the stitch. Some books will advise you to fill in a whole block with half crosses, then retrace your steps, completing the crosses for the whole block. I prefer to complete each row before going on to the next, but this is a matter of personal taste. One thing, however, is essential: that you always work the top stitch of each cross in the same direction.

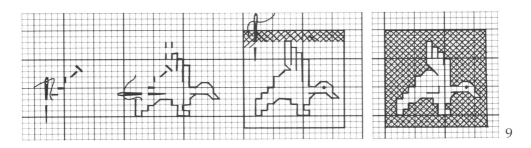

9

Embroiderers in Assisi always follow the order shown in fig. 9 which is the method described in all the text books. They first work the outlines and detail in Holbein stitch, then fill in the background with cross stitch. This can also be seen in the example in fig. 3 of an uncompleted design from the sixteenth century. In those days, this was the only possible solution, because the outlines of the motifs were drawn freely on to the material without reference to the weave. But in modern Assisi work the outlines are measured out on the grid of the material, so that both kinds of stitch must be carefully counted. This means that the design can be worked the other way round, which I personally prefer. I first embroider the crosses to form the background, and only then go on to do the outlines. This has the advantage that the outlines are embroidered on top of the cross stitches and so stand out more clearly. What is more, I find it much simpler to count out the cross stitches as I go, rather than having to work out carefully where the next running stitch for the outline is supposed to go. It is also much easier to spot a mistake.

THE DESIGNS

Given the correct technique, any cross-stitch design can be interpreted as an Assisi design, provided the 'negative' method is used – that is, the design is voided while the background is worked. Any cross-stitch design is suitable if it possesses well-defined outlines, and some beautiful modern interpretations of Assisi techniques are possible.

The designs which I have chosen for this book may not have come directly from the original 1902 collection, but all of them originated in Assisi during the first quarter of this century. I have not included the fauns and satyrs which were especially popular in the 1920s, because I cannot think of any suitable use for them today. But the traditional medieval motifs can still be used for the same purposes that they have served in Assisi from the turn of the century down to the present day: on tablecloths, cushion panels, place settings and napkins, for borders on clothing, and as emblems and monograms to suit every need.

As you leaf through the designs, you will immediately notice the voided motifs. But you should not forget the importance of the scrollwork that surrounds the designs, for each of these elements – the loose spirals of the scrollwork as much as the cross-stitch designs – is an essential feature of genuine Assisi embroidery. The scrollwork forms a soft edge to the main design, and helps to reduce the heavy and massive effect which it might otherwise give. It also serves to link the main designs on a tablecloth or other large piece of work. The scrollwork in Assisi embroidery forms a continuous border design, the elements of which are always interlinked, whether in a single running design or in an elaborate network of patterns. They never stand on their own as scattered motifs.

The scrollwork in Assisi embroidery comes most notably to the fore in those designs which at first glance are difficult to identify as Assisi work at all. In the designs shown in figs 84-94, the scrollwork is so dominant that the cross stitch no longer forms a background but becomes part of the scrollwork design.

The scrollwork patterns on either side of the border designs can easily be swapped if the necessity arises. If the scrollwork for a particular design is too wide or two narrow for the piece planned, then it can simply be replaced by that of a different design. The scrollwork above the border need not be of the same width as that below. But if they are of different widths, then the narrower or the looser scrollwork should always be above – or on the inside, in the case of a tablecloth.

COLOUR REQUIREMENTS

All Assisi embroidery is worked on white or natural-coloured cloth, and two colours of thread are used. First there is the background colour, which is used both for the cross-stitch background and for the scrollwork, making this the predominant colour in the design. Then there is the darker colour which is used for the outlines. The only exceptions to this rule are those small cross-stitch motifs which are included in a scrollwork design (see fig. 84). In such cases the Holbein stitch is in a dark colour – usually black – while the cross stitches are red or occasionally yellow.

The favourite colour combination for Assisi embroidery is red with black outline. The main colour can be blue or green, however, or more rarely gold. The outlines are occasionally embroidered in brown instead of black. If you choose blue or green for the main colour, then it should not be too dark, so that the outlines will stand out sufficiently.

HEMS

All the tablecloths and place settings from Assisi have decorative hems. The most usual form is a row of hemstitching with a second row of hemstitching immediately above it. Exactly as many threads should be drawn for each stitch as have been used for each cross stich in the background. The distance between the two rows should again be the same number of threads.

One special feature of Assisi embroidery which you may like to imitate is to be found on small tablecloths. At each corner of the cloth, three small loops are sewn into the holes left by the hemstitching. In each case the thread is sewn firmly to the hole, then wound four times through the hole and over the index finger. The resulting loop is then knotted directly round the hem itself, and finally the thread is firmly stitched down.

*   *   *   *   *

I hope you will enjoy following the patterns in this book, and that you will set about the work after the fashion of St Francis of Assisi himself – perhaps not religiously, but certainly with much enjoyment.

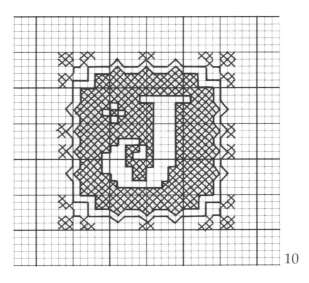

10

MEDALLIONS

The next few pages show a variety of medallion patterns of different sizes. They can either be used alone – on a napkin or a blouse pocket, for instance – or else placed in rows a greater or lesser distance apart. The medallions may also be connected by means of narrow bands of scrollwork, as in fig. 12.

Many different forms of medallion can be used – circles, ovals, hexagons, octagons, or even stars. But the shape of the medallion should be specifically chosen to match the motif which it contains. In fig. 11, for example, the vertical sides of the medallion match the design of the left-hand bird, while the tail feathers of the right-hand bird correspond to the step-like curves (characteristic of cross stitch) at the corners of the medallion. Similarly, the angle of the leaping monster motif in the lower medallion corresponds to the diagonal sides of the octagon. The pattern below right in fig. 18 shows a similar mythical beast in a different pose, in which the upraised paw serves to fill the top left-hand corner of the square.

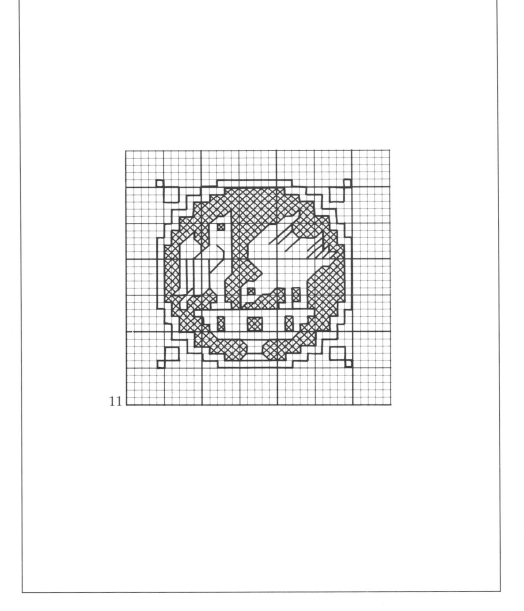

11

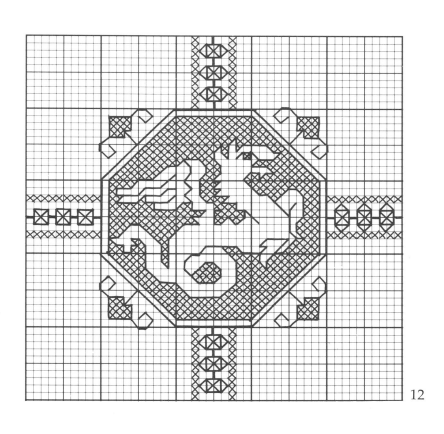

12

13

14

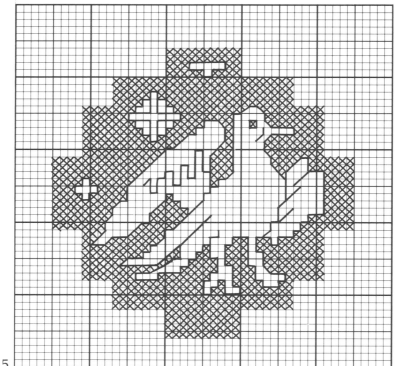

15

16

18

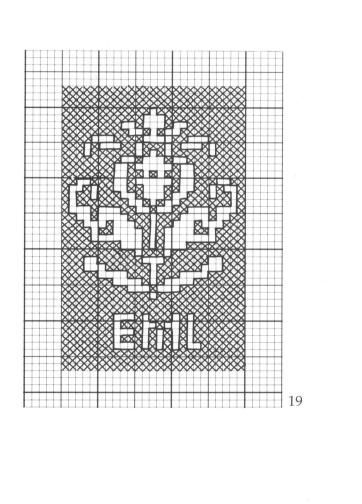

19

20

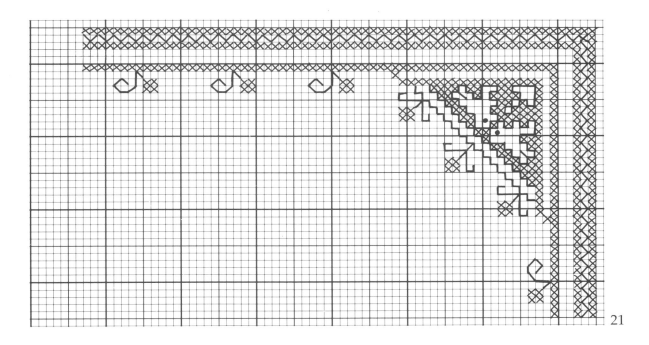

21

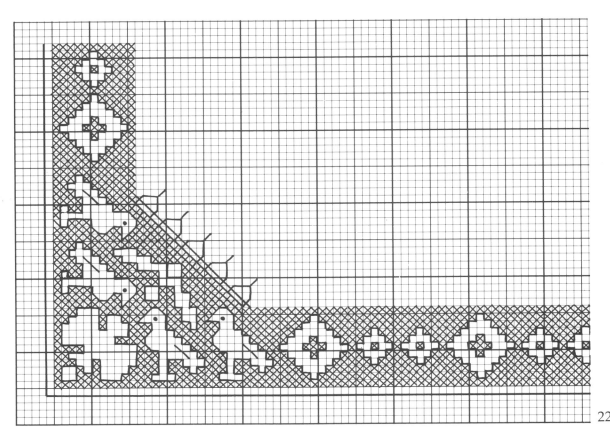

22

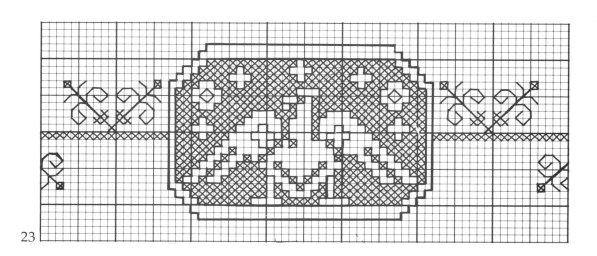

23

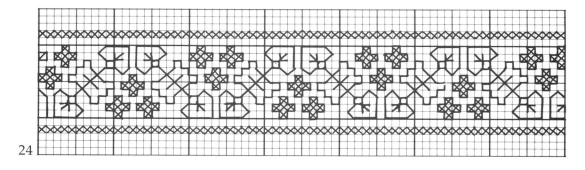

24

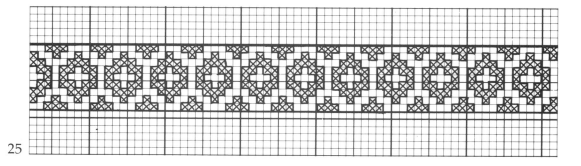

25

34

BIRD BORDERS

The animal pairs represented in figs 26-55 can be lined up in rows of any length you like. Assisi embroidery does use animals other than birds – deer, dogs, sea-horses, lions and hares – but birds are very much the favourite designs. There are a vast number of different bird motifs, including doves and ducks, swans and geese, and also a number of fabulous winged beasts.

As far as the scope of this book allows, I have tried to include the whole repeat of a design, incorporating both left and right member of each pair. But in cases such as the large border in fig. 27, it was impossible to get much more than half the repeat on to the page. However, since such animal pairs are invariably symmetrical, you should have no problem in working out the rest of the pattern. Once you have reached the middle of the design in the normal way – from left to right – until you reach the middle; then work a mirror image – that is, from right to left. To help you, I have sometimes indicated the beginning and the middle of the design with an **O** and an **M**, and then work backwards from **M** to **O**.

All the borders in Assisi embroidery must have scrollwork both above and below, which may be wider or narrower, denser or looser, depending on the actual design. Where the scrollwork either side of the border is symmetrical, I have sometimes shown only one side for reasons of space, and it should not be difficult to fill in the other.

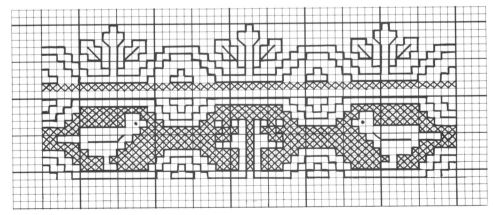

26

27

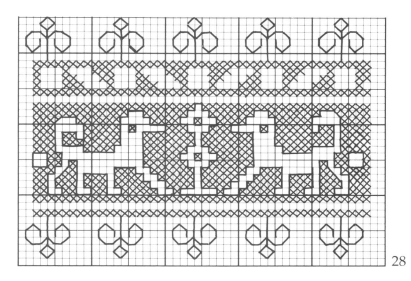

28

29

30

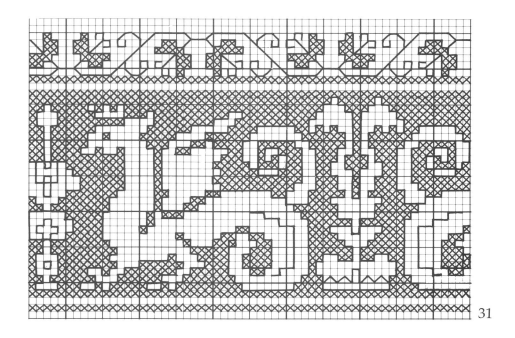

31

32

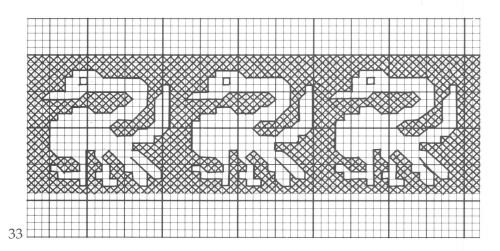

33

34

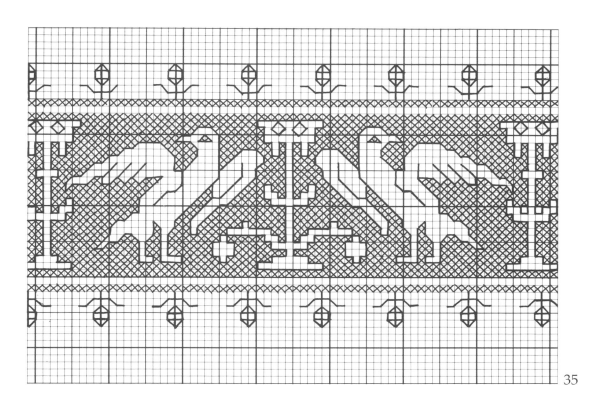

35

36

41

37

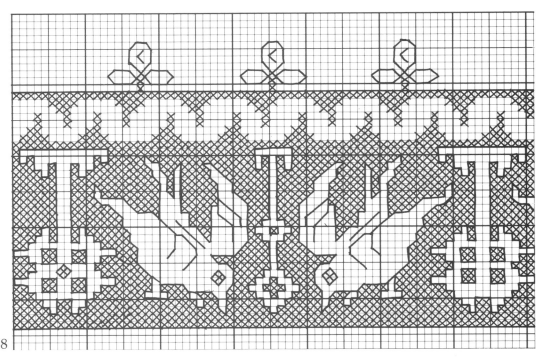

38

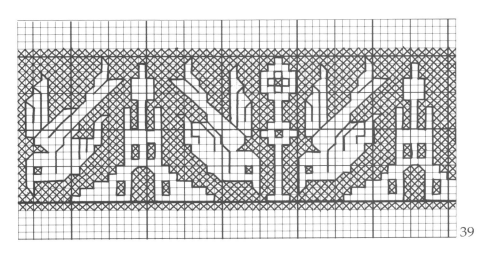

39

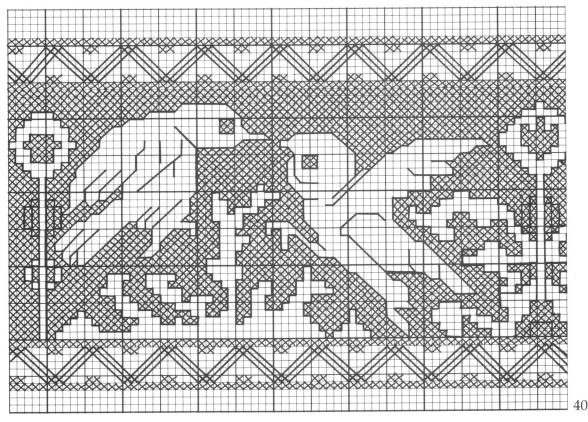

40

41

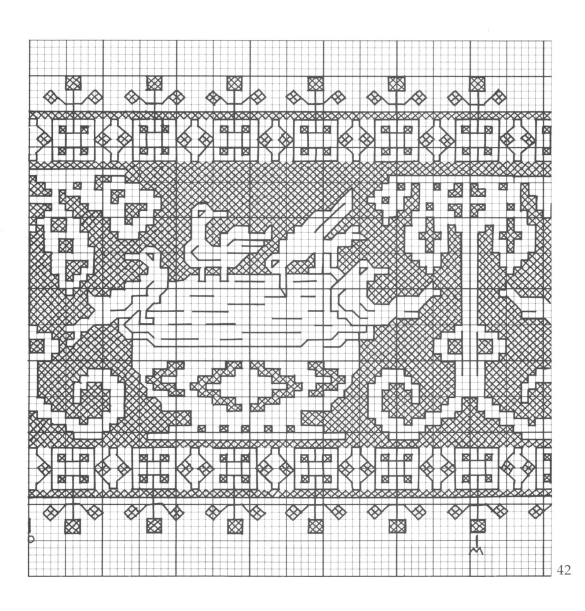

42

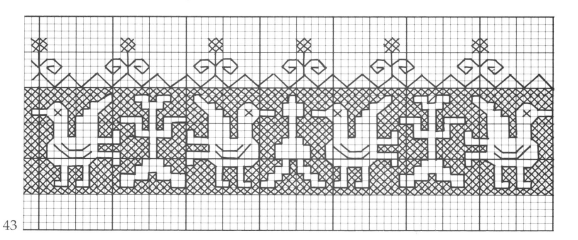

43

44

45

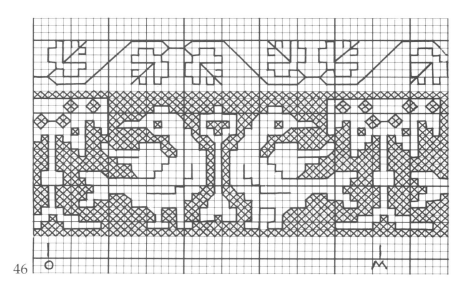

46

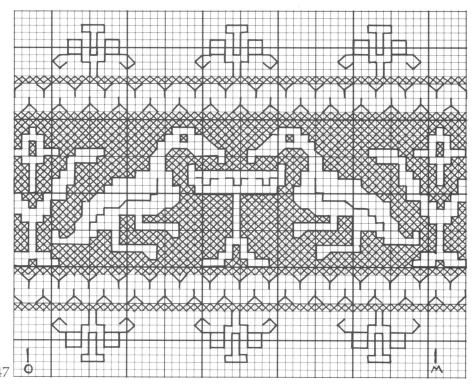

47

48

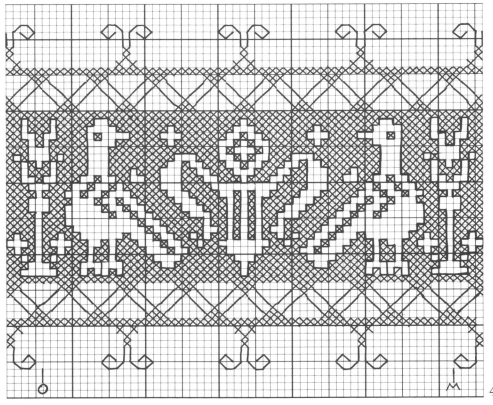

49

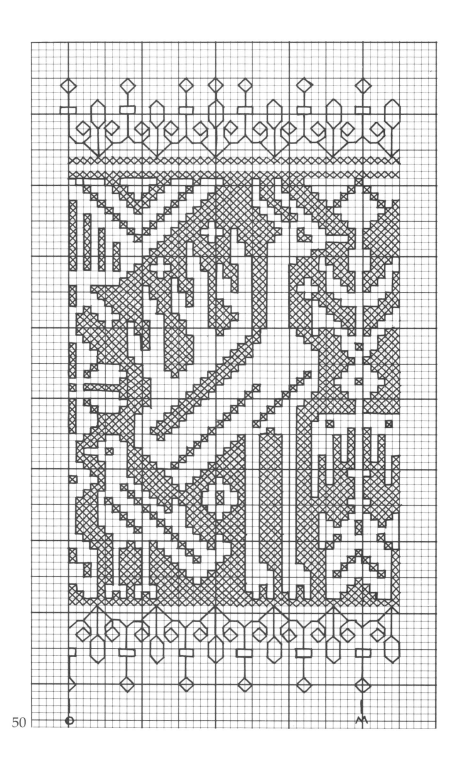

50

51

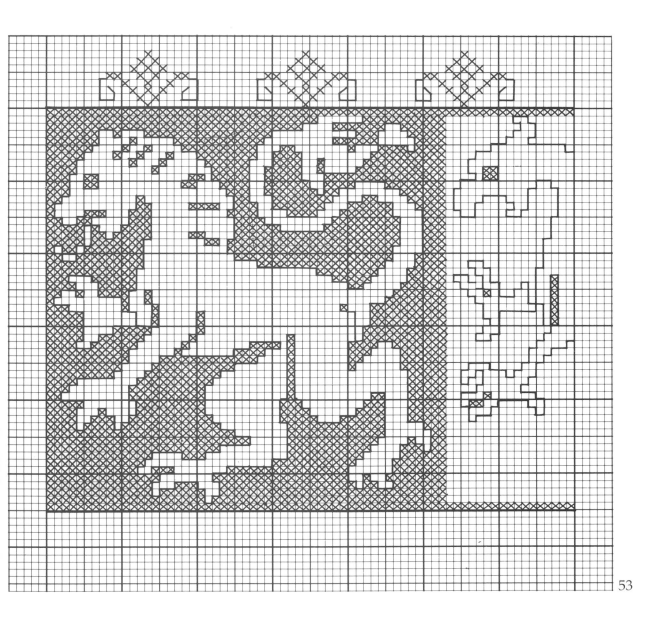

53

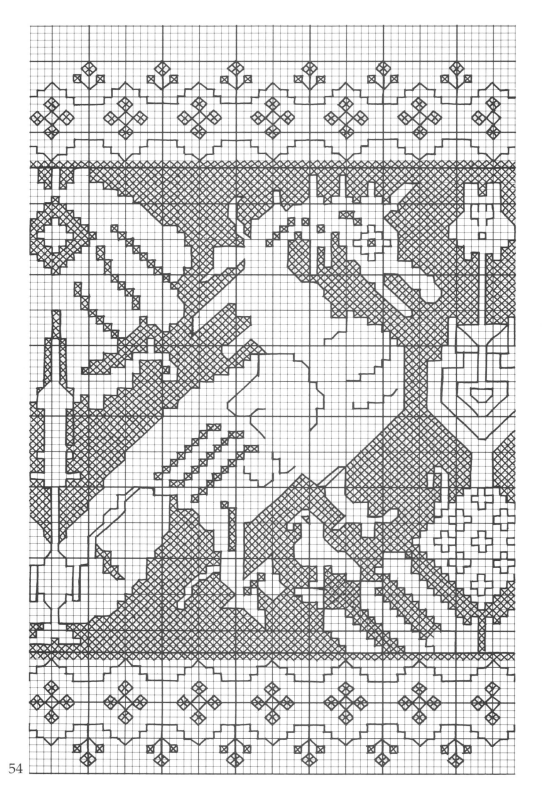

54

55

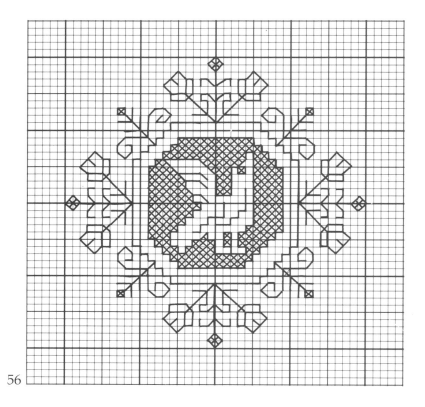

56

SCROLLWORK BORDERS

The medallions which appear here and in figs 10-18 may not only be joined together by means of narrow bands of scrollwork, but may also be combined with whole areas of filigree scrolling to form broad, spacious borders, as in fig. 57. On the other hand, the bird or bird-pair motifs in the borders may also reappear in medallions, as in figs 59 and 60.

Purely abstract motifs are rare in Assisi embroidery. But there are two particularly fine examples of this in the square ornamental designs in figs 61 and 62. Fig. 62 is the more austere, while fig. 61 shows a more playful floral design; the difference between them is further emphasized by the scrollwork. For a rather formal motif such as fig. 62, you might consider working the scrollwork in black like the outlines, and not in gold, as would normally be the case.

57

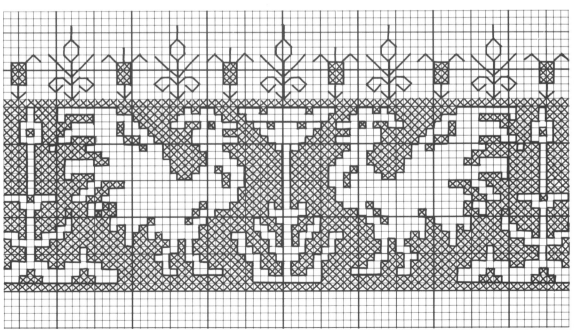

58

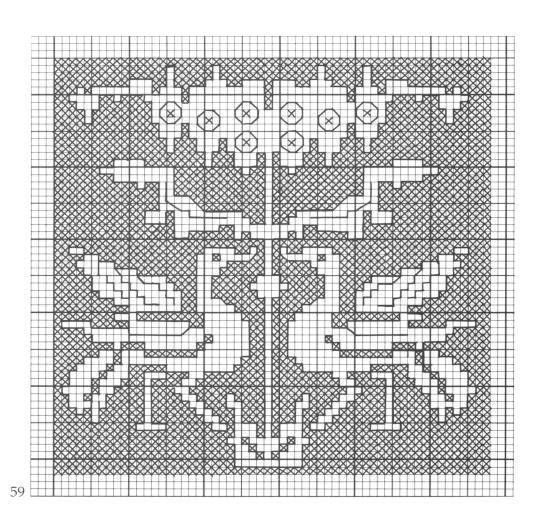

59

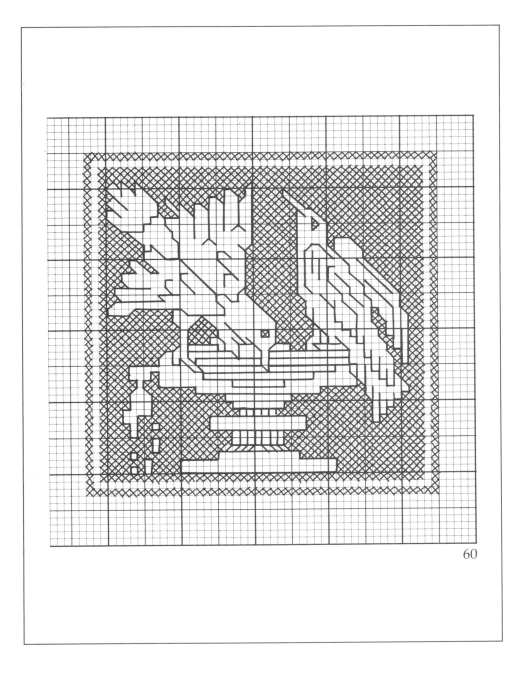

60

61

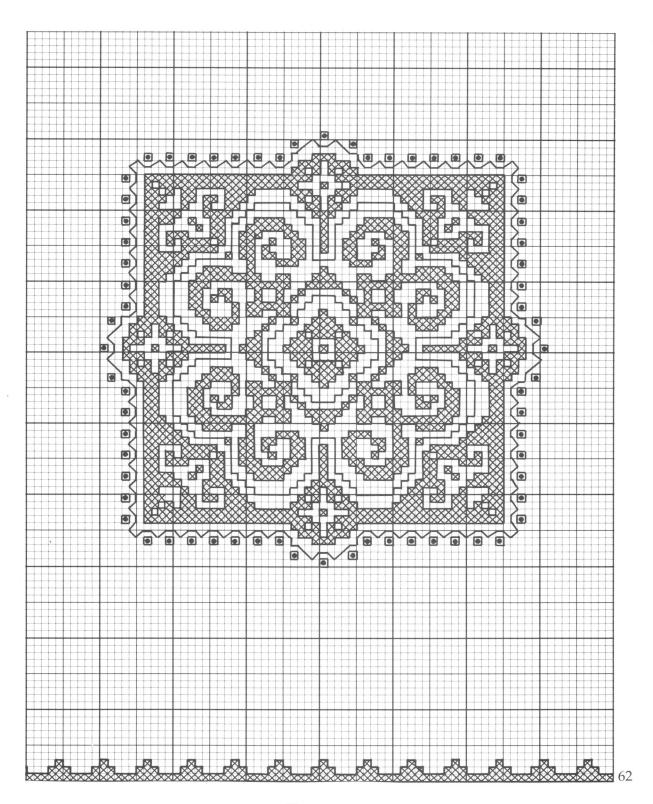

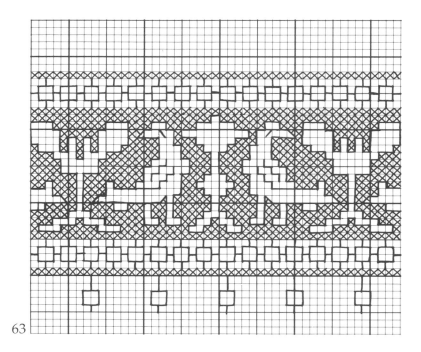

63

RUNNING BORDERS WITH CORNERS

Purely abstract motifs can be mirrored at any point in the design to give delightful corner designs, as in figs 67 and 68, whereas the paired animal motifs in traditional Assisi embroidery can be mirrored only in the middle or at the end of the design – that is, following the half-repeat of the design. With a fairly large motif, you may need to use a piece of fabric which is as much as 5 or even 10 cm (2-4 in.) longer or shorter than you originally planned.

Perhaps the nicest borders are those in which the animals look at each other round the corners, as in fig. 64, or those in which their heads come together, as with the swans in fig. 65. In both cases the design is mirrored from the middle. In the example in fig. 66, the design is mirrored at the end, so that the birds stretch their wings back to touch.

Although the design in fig. 68 is more abstract than the other examples, a suitable corner is possible only at the end of the repeat: but because the abstract part of the design is symmetrical both ways, it does not need to be mirrored.

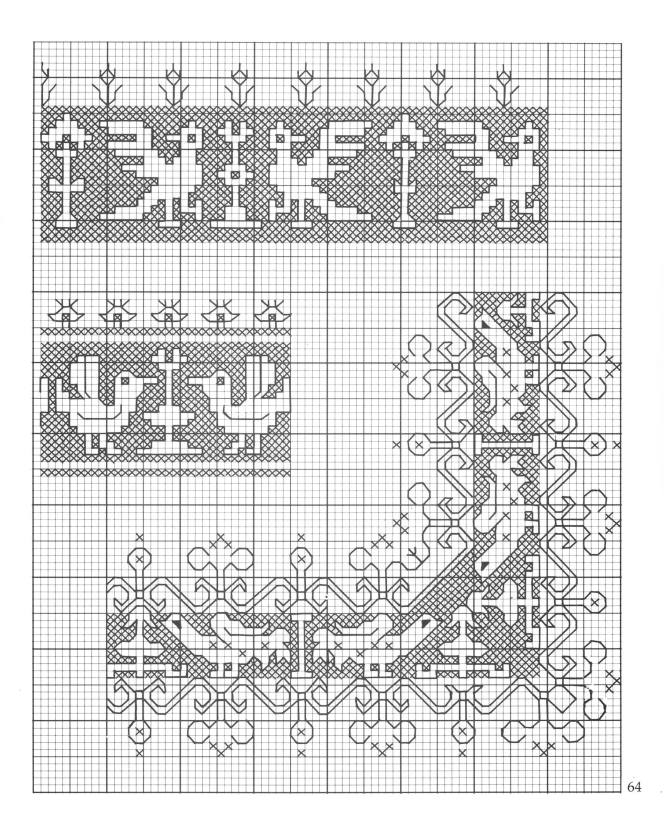

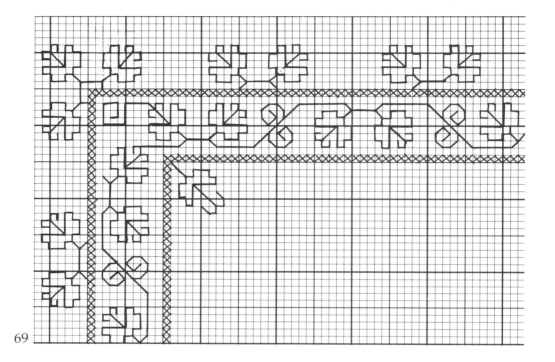

69

MEDALLION CLOTHS

In Assisi embroidery, cross-stitch medallions are used not only as single emblems, but are more often incorporated into large tablecloth designs. The rather heavy medallions are joined together with filigree scrollwork and embroidered as borders around the edges of the cloth. The medallions are placed symmetrically either side of a central medallion on each of the four sides. The distance from each corner to the adjacent medallions is determined by the size of the medallions, which are not allowed to touch if they are on adjoining edges of the cloth. If several medallion borders are placed one inside another, then the medallions in the second row are placed centrally between those in the first, and so on.

The distance between adjacent medallions on one cloth must always be the same, but the length of the connecting scrollwork can always be varied to accommodate the design to cloths of different sizes.

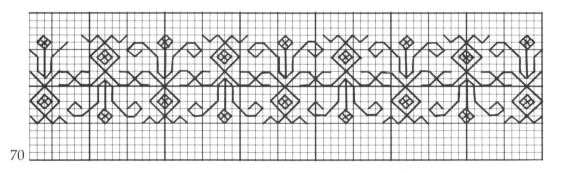

70

72

Assisi embroidery often uses the same animal motifs for different purposes. Fig. 72 shows an example of a sea-horse pair, which is widely spaced as a border motif, while it is crowded closer together in fig. 73 to form the medallion for a large tablecloth.

There are many more examples of motifs that have been re-used with only slight modifications in various border, medallion or corner designs.

A second row need not contain medallions, but many simply consist of the running scrollwork design. This means that it may be placed much nearer to the outer border, as is shown in the example opposite. Or it may be placed much nearer the centre of the cloth to form a wreath – another form of decoration which is frequently used in Assisi embroidery.

73

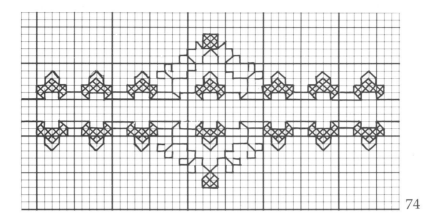

74

CORNER DESIGNS

The second most common Assisi design, after the medallion cloth, is one which emphasizes the corners. In this case the cross-stitch design may appear only at the corners of the cloth, and is connected by means of scrollwork.

Depending on the size of the cloth, the design may either be represented at all four corners, or appear at two diagonally opposite corners, or even at one corner only. The scrollwork should run along the border of the whole cloth, even when only one corner is emphasized.

Shown in fig. 75 is one of the most beautiful corner designs I have ever found in Assisi embroidery – a tree full of birds extending far in towards the centre of the cloth, guarded on either side by a pair of swans. The simple scrollwork pattern (see fig. 74 above) merges modestly into the background beside the much larger main design. The scrollwork may connect this corner with the other corners; but if it is a single corner design, then the scrollwork will simply run round the whole of the cloth and back to this corner.

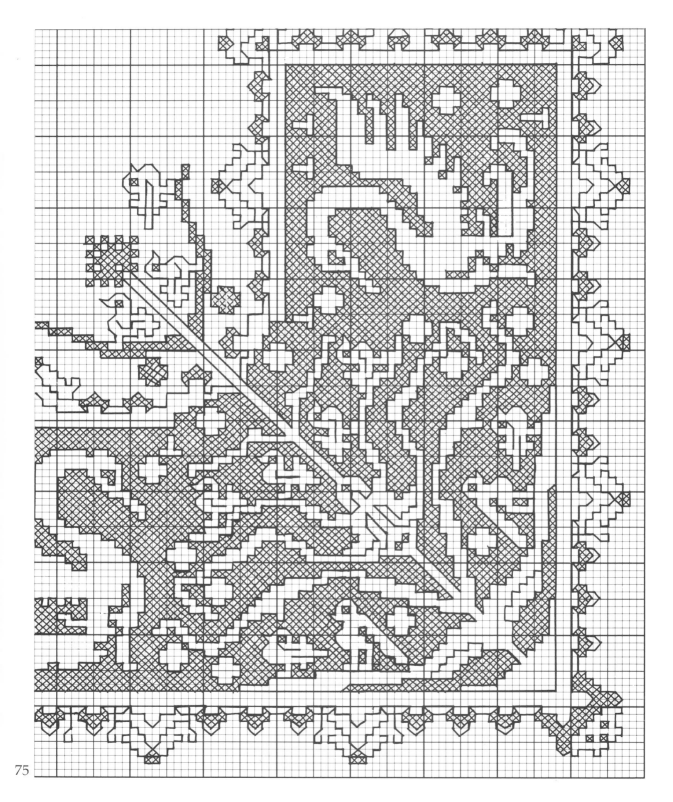

75

76

In contrast to fig. 25, in which the corner design cuts off rather abruptly, in fig. 77 it tapers off more slowly as shown in fig. 76, merging gently into the scrollwork. As in all cloth designs, further rows of scrollwork may be incorporated, or else the second row of scrollwork may lead directly into another corner design. The latter option might be used to create a small but richly embroidered cloth design, or a beautiful cushion panel.

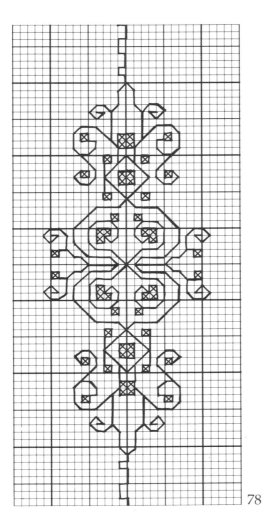

78

In Assisi embroidery, not all corner designs are made up of large border elements, as in the examples shown so far. They may also incorporate smaller, more modest border motifs, such as the pair of little hares in fig. 79, which is simply mirrored at the corner. An especially nice feature is the way the scrollwork pattern (figs 78 and 79) encloses the ends of the corner design.

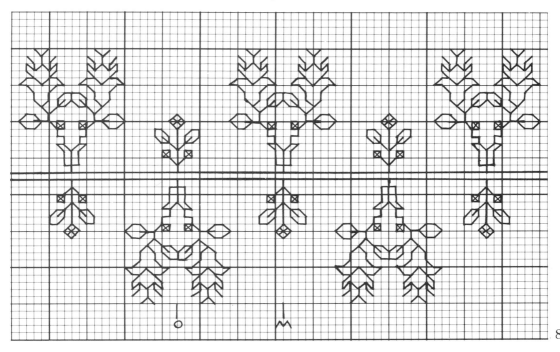

80

Fig. 80 is a particularly clear example of a double scrollwork design which not only serves to link the corner designs, but also then divides to run either side of each corner design.

The bird pond in fig. 81 is a very popular traditional motif. In fig. 42 it is incorporated into a border and is almost oval in shape. Here it is more trapezoid in form, echoing the pointed ends of the corner design. The little birds drinking show clearly how much finer the detail can be in Assisi embroidery than in more conventional cross-stitch designs. If cross stitch alone were used, it would be impossible to show the same detail of wings, eyes, feet and feathers for such tiny birds.

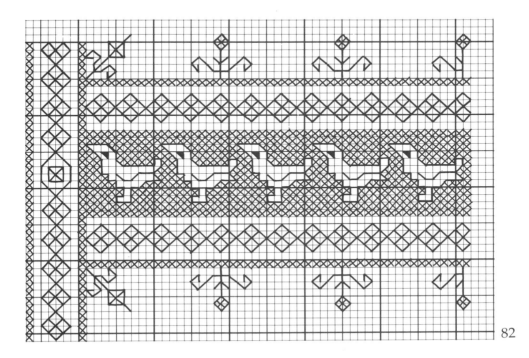

82

The square emblem in fig. 83 is linked not by scrollwork but by a heavier border design (fig. 82). Just look at the beautiful way the border has been developed, using dove motifs that continue round the edge of the corner design.

Linking the corners by means of a border is a good solution here. Soft scrollwork would have paled into insignificance beside such a powerful corner motif, and would have been ineffective as a linking device.

If worked on anything but the finest linen, this dove emblem would be, in my view, rather too large and heavy for the corner of a tablecloth. But the bird border could also be used alone to edge a tablecloth, while the main design is highly suitable for a cushion panel or wall hanging.

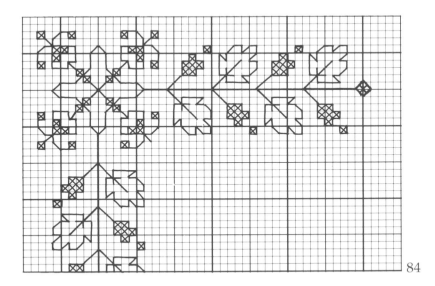

84

SCROLLWORK DESIGNS

When first you look at these designs, you may easily confuse the oakleaf pattern with the scrollwork in figs 71-3. But there is a vital difference between them. The design on this page is embroidered in cross stitch as well as in Holbein stitch, and is therefore in two colours. The diamond patterns bear no resemblance to the medallions in figs. 71-3, for even inside the diamonds, Holbein stitch and cross stitch are of equal importance in forming the design, and no actual object is represented.

After medallion cloths and cloths with large corner motifs, this form of scrollwork embroidery is the third most important category of Assisi embroidery. In these designs, both the outlines and also the scrollwork are embroidered in black. The little red crosses are distributed individually throughout the scrollwork. Although only two colours are used, the overall effect is of much more colour than with the other types of Assisi embroidery.

The design in fig. 85 is worked in the manner shown across the whole area of the cloth. A more modest variant of the design may be used (fig. 84) as a corner design to link some of the diamonds.

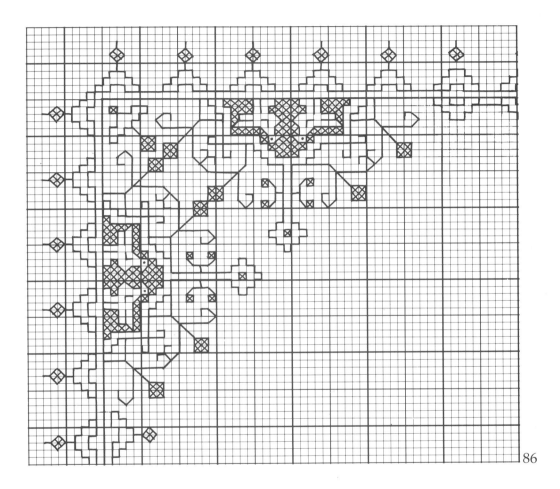

86

The design in fig. 87 is a particularly colourful one. No matter whether the cross stitch is red or gold, it will always contrast brightly against the black scrollwork and the black outlines of the comical bird motifs.

The design in fig. 88 may be used either as a border or as an area design, as shown in the top left-hand corner. The cheeky little birds make this an ideal design for children. If the little circles are filled with a more abstract design, the effect is somewhat more sober!

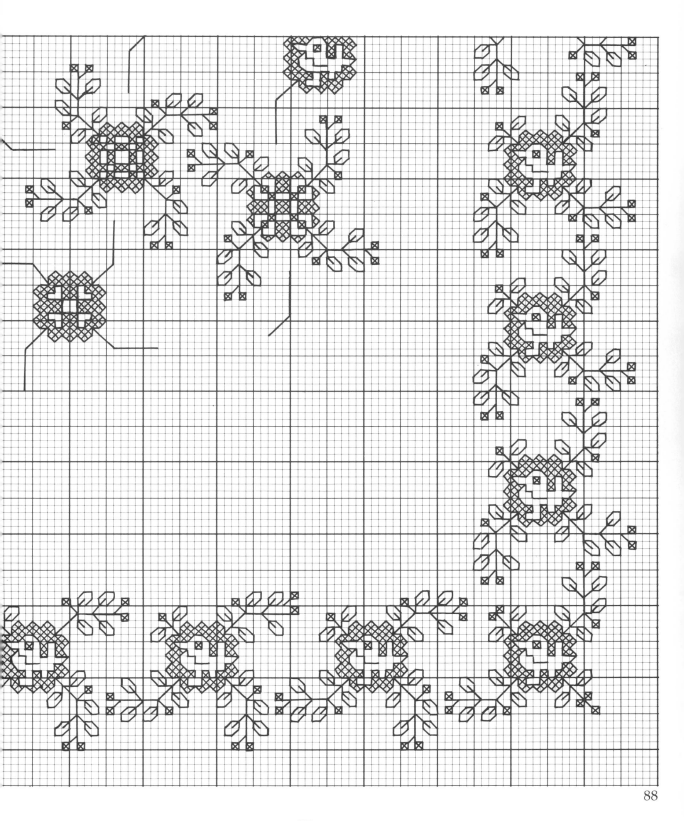

REPEAT

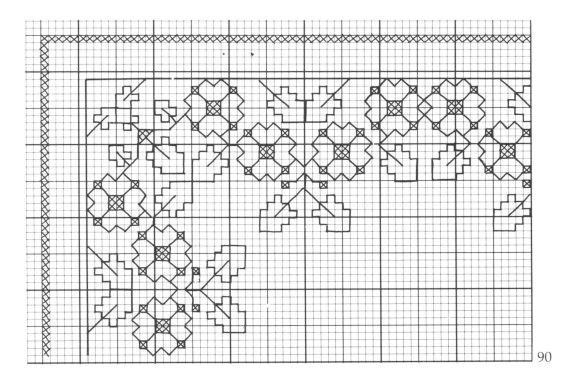

90

Designs like those in figs 90 and 91 are nearly always embroidered in black Holbein stitch and red cross stitch. The writing along the edge is worked in ordinary cross stitch. At first glance this might seem unusual, since it is apparently not a genuine Assisi technique. However, this kind of edging is frequently used in designs with softer-looking scrollwork. The narrow cross-stitch border frames the filigree design very effectively without smothering it.

The design in fig. 89 is quite different. Here a narrow red cross-stitch border forms the boundary between a broader and a narrower scrollwork pattern. The scrollwork is interspersed with small cross-stitch motifs looking rather like tiny flowers or fruit, which serve to offset the rigidity of the cross-stitch border itself. This means that the border can be worked according to the more usual pattern of outlines and background.

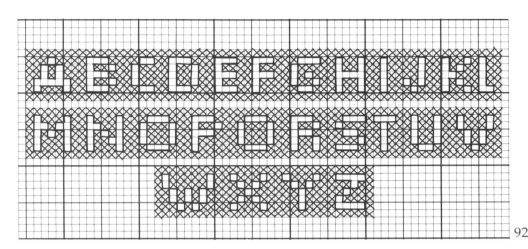

92

ALPHABETS AND LETTERING

Like the example in fig. 91, the design in fig. 93 is again bordered by ordinary cross stitches. The alphabetic design from which the letters in the border have been formed is shown in voided form in fig. 92. This means that if you wish you can embroider the border in fig. 89 with a quote or a proverb instead of the bird motifs. If you examine the initials under the pomegranate in fig. 19, you will see that they have been taken from the same alphabet.

The sampler in fig. 94 does not come from Assisi at all, but is one that I have developed from a typeface. Its clarity makes it highly suitable for Assisi embroidery. The letters are easy to read, and are therefore admirably suited to monogram medallions such as those shown in figs. 10 and 19. The last design in the book (fig. 95), is, as you might expect, a depiction of St Francis himself, surrounded by little birds and the legendary wolf.

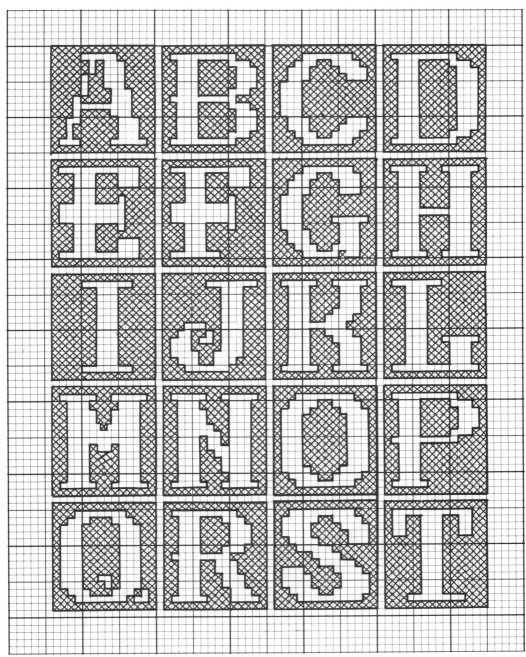

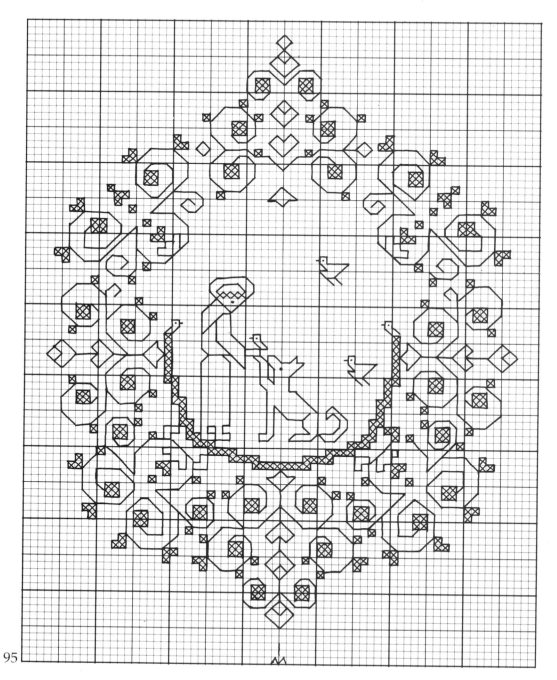

LIST OF SUPPLIERS

UK

Creative Crafts
11 The Square
Winchester
SO23 9ES
(General embroidery supplies)

Handworker's Market
18 Chapel Yard
Albert Street
Holt
Norfolk
(General embroidery supplies)

Hepatica
82a Water Lane
Wilmslow
Cheshire
(General embroidery supplies)

The Irish Linen Depot
39 Bond Street
Ealing
London
W5 5AS
*(Linens and general
embroidery supplies)*

L. Lockhart & Son Ltd
Linktown Works
Kirkaldy
Fife
Scotland
(Linens)

Mace & Nairn
89 Crane Street
Salisbury
Wiltshire
SP1 2PY
(General embroidery supplies)

Christine Riley
53 Barclay Street
Stonehaven
Kincardineshire
AB3 2AR
(General embroidery supplies)

Royal School of Needlework
25 Princes Gate
London
SW7 1QE
(General embroidery supplies)

Thread wholesalers
(write for list of stockists)

Coats Anchor Threads
Marketing Services Dept
Coats Domestic Marketing
Division
39 Durham Street
Glasgow
G41 1BS

DMC UK Distributors
Dunlicraft Ltd
Pullman Road
Wigston
Leicester
LE8 2DY

Gutermann-Perivale
Wadsworth Road
Greenford
Middlesex
UB6 7JS

USA

American Crewel
and Canvas Studio
164 Canal Street
Canastota
NY 13032

Counted Thread
3305 S. Newport Street
Denver
CO 80224

The Needlecraft Shop
PO Box 1406
Canoga Park
CA 91304

The World in Stitches
PO Box 198
Osgood Roda
Milford
NH 03055

Thread wholesalers
(write for list of stockists)

Susan Bates Inc.
PO Box E
Route 9A
212 Middlesex Avenue
Chester
CT 06412

DMC Corporation
107 Trumbell Street
Elizabeth
NJ 07206

OTHER BATSFORD EMBROIDERY BOOKS

CROSS STITCH PATTERNS
Irmgard Gierl

A superb collection of traditional patterns, ranging from small motifs and borders to full-scale designs. Gathered from Germany, Switzerland, Austria and Romania, these will make delightful decorations for clothes, fashion accessories and household linen.
88 pages
40 pages of patterns
ISBN 0 7134 5418 0

DRAWN FABRIC EMBROIDERY
Edna Wark

Looks at the history of this counted thread technique before going on to assess its potential for modern work. Subjects covered include: design, stitches, technique, planning embroideries, drawn fabric work on dress, making small items, and finishing articles.
144 pages
116 illustrations
ISBN 0 7134 1477 4

CROSS STITCH SAMPLERS
Jane Kendon

Shows you how to create samplers as charming as those worked by children in the past. Many charted designs are provided, together with advice on colours and techniques.
120 pages
60 illustrations
ISBN 0 7134 4917 9

BLACKWORK EMBROIDERY
Margaret Pascoe

For all embroiderers wishing to know more about this elegant and historic type of work. The author explains the techniques used and shows how to develop your own designs.
144 pages
over 150 illustrations
ISBN 0 7134 5145 9

For a complete list of Batsford embroidery books, please write to:

B.T. Batsford Ltd
4 Fitzhardinge Street
London
W1H 0AH